Budget Bites

igloo

Published by Igloo Books Ltd
Cottage Farm
Sywell
NN6 0BJ
www.igloo-books.com

10 9 8 7 6 5 4 3 2 1

ISBN: 978 1 84852 724 9

Project Managed by R&R Publications Marketing Pty Ltd

Food Photography: R&R Photostudio (www.rrphotostudio.com.au)
Recipe Development: R&R Test Kitchen

Front cover photograph © Stockfook/Tanya Zouey

Printed in and manufactured in China

Contents

Minestrone Soup with Soda Bread

Preparation 30 mins **Cooking** 40 mins **Calories** 775

1 tbsp vegetable oil
6 slices rindless lean bacon, chopped
1 onion, chopped
2 cloves garlic, chopped
150g (5oz) carrots, sliced thinly
1 leek, sliced thinly
250g (9oz) potatoes, peeled chopped
5 cups vegetable stock
2 tbsp tomato paste
60g (2oz) dried spaghetti
salt and black pepper

Soda Bread

250g (9oz) wholewheat flour
250g (9oz) flour
½ tsp salt
1 tsp baking soda
60g (2oz) chilled butter, cubed
2 tbsp chopped fresh parsley
juice of ½ lemon
1 cup whole milk

Soda Bread

1 Preheat the oven to 200°C (400°F.) Put the wholewheat flour into a bowl, then sift in the flour, salt and baking soda, mixing well. Rub in the butter until the mixture resembles coarse breadcrumbs. Mix in the parsley. Add the lemon juice to the milk and stir into the flour mixture to form a soft but not sticky dough.

2 Punch down the dough lightly on a floured surface and flatten slightly into a 20cm (8in) round. Place on a baking sheet and cut a cross into the top. Cook at the top of the oven for 35–40 minutes, until well risen and golden.

Soup

1 Heat the oil in a largew saucepan. Add the bacon, onion, garlic, carrot, leeks and potato and cook for 5 minutes or until softened. Stir in the stock and tomato paste, then simmer, covered, for 20 minutes, or until all the vegetables have softened. Break the spaghetti into 2½cm (1in) lengths and add to the pan. Cook for 10 minutes or until the pasta is tender but still firm to the bite. Season to taste and serve with the bread.

Serves 4

Rutabaga and Carrot Soup

Preparation 5 mins **Cooking** 45 mins **Calories** 49

1 medium onion, diced

1 tbsp oil

1 rutabaga, peeled and chopped (about 2 cups)

2 small carrots, peeled and chopped

salt to taste

1 cup vegetable stock

½ tsp ground ginger

¼ tsp ground nutmeg

2 cups fresh orange juice

ground black pepper to taste

1 Sauté the onion in oil for 5 minutes.

2 Add the carrot, rutabaga, salt and the pepper. Sauté for 10 minutes, stirring occasionally.

3 Add the vegetable stock and cook covered over low heat for 20–30 minutes until the vegetables are tender.

4 Add spices. Purée in a blender with the orange juice. Reheat and serve.

Serves 4

Roasted Pepper with Herbs

Preparation 10 mins **Cooking** 45 mins **Calories** 85

3 red peppers
2 green peppers
4 medium fresh green chilies
2 onions, quartered
2 tbsp fresh marjoram leaves
2 tbsp fresh thyme leaves
3 tbsp lime juice
3 tbsp olive oil
freshly ground black pepper

1 Place the red and green peppers and chilies in a hot skillet and cook until skins are blistered and charred. Place peppers and chilies in a plastic food bag and stand for 10 minutes or until cool enough to handle.

2 Carefully remove skins from the peppers and chilies, then cut off tops and remove seeds and membranes. Cut into thick slices.

3 Place the onions in the skillet and cook for 5 minutes or until soft and charred.

4 Place the peppers, chilies, onions, marjoram, thyme, lime juice, oil and black pepper to taste in a bowl and toss to combine. Stand for 30 minutes before serving.

Serves 6

Asparagus and Salmon Salad

Preparation 15 mins **Cooking** 5 mins **Calories** 69

750g (1¾lb) asparagus spears, trimmed

lettuce leaves of your choice

500g (18oz) smoked salmon slices

freshly ground black pepper

Lemon Yogurt Sauce

200g (7oz) natural low-fat yogurt

1 tbsp finely grated lemon zest

1 tbsp lemon juice

1 tbsp chopped fresh dill

1 tsp ground cumin

1 Boil, steam or microwave asparagus until tender. Drain, refresh under cold running water, drain again and chill. Arrange lettuce leaves, asparagus and salmon on serving plates. Spoon sauce over salad. Sprinkle with black pepper, cover and chill until required.

Lemon Yogurt Sauce

1 Place yogurt, lemon rind, lemon juice, dill and cumin in a small bowl and mix to combine.

Serves 4

Variation: Try 400g (14oz) green beans and 400g (14oz) snowpeas instead of asparagus spears.

Spinach and Chicken Omelet Baguettes
Preparation 15 mins **Cooking** 15 mins **Calories** 313

4 medium eggs
½ tsp salt
1 tsp sugar
1 tbsp vegetable oil, plus extra for brushing
1 skinless boneless chicken breast, cut into very thin strips
1 clove garlic, crushed
250g (9oz) fresh spinach, shredded
60g (2oz) bean sprouts
2 tsp light soy sauce
4 small baguettes, cut in half lengthways

1 Break the eggs into a bowl, add the salt and sugar and beat lightly. Heat a 20cm (8in) heavy-based skillet and lightly brush with oil. Pour in a quarter of the egg mixture and swirl to coat the bottom of the pan. Cook for 1½ minutes or until the omelet is set and golden on the base, then turn over and cook for 30 seconds more or until cooked through. Remove from the pan and keep warm. Cook the remaining 3 omelets in the same way.

2 Heat 1 tablespoon of oil in the skillet, add the chicken strips and garlic, then cook for 3 minutes or until the chicken is cooked through. Add the spinach and bean sprouts and cook for 1–2 minutes, until the spinach starts to wilt. Sprinkle with soy sauce.

3 Top each omelette with a quarter of the chicken and spinach mixture. Roll up and place in a baguette, then serve immediately.

Serves 4

Falafel in Pita Bread with Salad

Preparation 25 mins **Cooking** 10 mins **Calories** 54

400g (14oz) can chickpeas, drained

1 small onion, finely chopped

1–2 cloves garlic, crushed

1 small red chili, deseeded and finely chopped

½ tsp ground cumin

1 tbsp chopped fresh cilantro

fresh lemon juice

1 medium egg, lightly beaten

3 tbsp flour

vegetable oil for frying

4 pita breads

shredded lettuce

chopped tomatoes

strained plain yogurt

black pepper to serve

1 Blend the chickpeas, onions, garlic, chili, cumin and cilantro in a blender to form a coarse paste. If the mixture is too dry to shape, add a little lemon juice.

2 Use your hands to shape the chickpea mixture into 20 balls, each about the size of a walnut. Dip into the beaten egg, then toss lightly in the flour. Heat 1cm (⅓in) of oil in a deep heavy-based skillet and fry half the batch of falafel for 3–4 minutes, turning, until crisp and golden. Drain well on kitchen towels and keep warm while you cook the second batch.

3 Slice open each pita bread, half fill with lettuce and tomatoes, then add 5 falafel. Top with a spoonful of yogurt and a sprinkling of black pepper.

Serves 4

Note: These spicy little chickpea patties are the Middle East's most popular snack. They make a great filling for pita bread, especially when topped with salad and yogurt.

Moroccan Lemon Chicken Shish Kebabs

Preparation 20 mins **Cooking** 20 mins **Calories** 117 per kebab

500g (18oz) skinless chicken breast fillets, trimmed of visible fat, cut into 25mm (1in) cubes

1 quantity red capsicum harissa (optional)

Moroccan Lemon Marinade

1 tbsp chopped fresh parsley

1 tbsp fresh rosemary leaves or 2 tsp dried rosemary

2 tsp fresh thyme or 1 tsp dried thyme

1 clove garlic, crushed

1 tsp crushed black peppercorns

grated zest and juice of 1 lemon or 1 preserved lemon

1 tbsp olive oil

Red Capsicum Harissa

2 red capsicums, cut in half lengthways, seeds removed

1 plum tomato, cut in half lengthways, seeds removed

1 tsp red wine vinegar

2 tsp tomato paste

hot chili sauce

freshly ground black pepper

Moroccan Lemon Marinade

1 Place parsley, rosemary, thyme, garlic, black pepper, lemon juice and zest and oil in a non-reactive bowl. Add chicken. Toss to combine. Cover. Marinate in the refrigerator for at least 30 minutes.

Kebabs

1 Preheat barbecue or broiler to a high heat. If using bamboo skewers, soak in cold water for at least 20 minutes.

2 Thread chicken onto skewers. Place on barbecue grill or under broiler. Cook, brushing frequently with marinade and turning, for 6–10 minutes or until chicken is cooked. Serve with red capsicum harissa for dipping.

Red Capsicum Harissa

1 Preheat the broiler to hot. Using your hands, flatten capsicum and tomato halves and place skin side up on aluminum foil under broiler. Cook until skins blacken. When cool remove skins.

2 Place the capsicum and tomato flesh in a food processor then add other ingredients to taste. Purée. Set aside until ready to serve.

Makes 8 kebabs

Pork Apple Parcels

Preparation 12 mins **Cooking** 30 mins **Calories** 177

1kg (2¼lb) lean pork schnitzel, trimmed of visible fat, pounded until very thin

2 apples, chopped

½ cup golden raisins

juice of ½ lemon

½ cup plum sauce

½ cup apple juice

1 tbsp soy sauce

1 tbsp honey

1 Preheat oven to 180°C (350°F).

2 Cut pork into 10cm (4in) squares. Set aside.

3 Place apples, golden raisins and lemon juice in a bowl. Mix to combine. Spread each pork square with plum sauce to within 2cm (1in) of the edges. Place a small mound of the apple mixture in the centre. Roll up to form a parcel. Tie with cooking string. Place in an ovenproof dish.

4 Combine apple juice, soy sauce and honey. Pour over pork parcels. Cover loosely with aluminium foil. Bake for 20–25 minutes or until pork is browned and tender. Remove parcels from dish.

5 Stir 2 tablespoons of the plum sauce into the cooking juices. Serve with parcels, for dipping.

Makes 12 parcels

Lamb Burger Pizza with Onion Topping

Preparation 25 mins **Cooking** 30 mins **Calories** 472

1 tbsp olive oil, plus extra for greasing

1 large tomato

500g (18oz) lean ground lamb

1 tsp mild chili powder

1 tsp Italian herb seasoning

1 small egg

125g (4oz) fresh white breadcrumbs

1 onion, coarsely chopped

1 clove garlic, crushed

2 tsp superfine sugar

½ tsp dried thyme

145g (5oz) ball mozzarella cheese, sliced

Alternative: to make this recipe a Turkey burger pizza with onion topping, substitute ground lamb with 500g (18oz) ground turkey meat.

1 Preheat the oven to 190°C (350°F). Lightly oil a 23cm (9in) pizza tin or flan dish. Put the tomato into a bowl and cover with boiling water. Leave for 30 seconds, then drain, peel and slice.

2 Put the ground lamb, chili powder, herb seasoning, egg and breadcrumbs into a bowl and mix well. Transfer to the pizza tin or flan dish and press with the back of a wooden spoon to cover the base. Bake for 25 minutes or until cooked through. Drain off any excess juices.

3 Meanwhile, make the topping. Heat the oil, add the onion and garlic and cook gently for 6 minutes or until softened. Add the sugar and thyme and cook for 10 minutes or until the onions have caramelized.

4 Preheat the broiler to high. Spread the onions over the burger and arrange the cheese and tomato slices over the top. Broiler for 3–5 minutes, until the cheese has just melted. Serve cut into large wedges.

Serves 4

Note: A cross between a burger and a pizza, this is sure to please children. They'll love it served with french fries or mashed potatoes. You can make individual pizzas if you prefer.

Lamb Hotpot Cooked in Cider

Preparation 25 mins **Cooking** 2 hrs 35 mins **Calories** 588

2 tbsp olive oil

4 loin lamb chops

6 lamb's kidneys, halved with skins and cores removed

1 onion, sliced

700g (1½lb) potatoes, sliced

2 carrots, sliced

1 large leek, sliced

2 celery stalks, sliced

salt and black pepper

3 sprigs fresh marjoram or oregano

1⅕ cups dry cider

1 Preheat the oven to 180°C (350°F). Heat one tablespoon of the oil in a large heavy-based skillet. Add the chops and cook for 1–2 minutes each side, until browned. Remove from the pan, then add the kidneys and cook for 30 seconds on each side or until lightly browned.

2 Arrange ½ the onion and potatoes in the base of an ovenproof dish. Top with the chops; add ½ the carrots, leek and celery, then the kidneys. Add the rest of the carrots, leek and celery, seasoning each layer well. Finish with a layer of onions and potatoes, then tuck in the marjoram or oregano sprigs. Pour over the cider and brush the top with the remaining oil.

3 Cover and cook for 1½–2 hours, until the meat is tender. Remove the lid, place near the top of the oven and cook for 20–30 minutes, until brown.

Serves 4

Sparerib Chops with Red Cabbage and Apples

Preparation 20 mins **Cooking** 1 hr 40 mins **Calories** 482

2 tbsp vegetable oil

4 large pork spare rib chops

1 onion, chopped

500g (18oz) red cabbage, finely shredded

500g (18oz) cooking apples, peeled, cored and thinly sliced

1 cup red wine or vegetable stock

salt and black pepper

parsley to garnish

1 Preheat the oven to 180°C (350°F). Heat the oil in a large flameproof dish. Add the spare rib chops and cook for 1½–2 minutes on each side, until lightly browned. Remove and keep warm. Add the onion and cook for another 5 minutes or until softened and golden.

2 Sir in the cabbage, apples and wine or stock. Season to taste. Place the pork chops on top and cover tightly. Cook in the oven for 1¼–1½ hours, until the pork is tender (you may need to add a little more wine or stock during cooking if the dish starts to dry out). Serve garnished with the parsley.

Serves 4

Note: The sweet and sour flavor of red cabbage and apples is perfect with pork. Make sure you buy the meatier spare rib chops and not plain ribs. Serve with mashed potatoes.

Steak and Kidney Pie

Preparation 20 mins **Cooking** 3 hrs **Calories** 250

1kg (2¼lb) lean topside steak,
cut into 25mm (1in) cubes

6 lamb's kidneys or 1 ox
kidney,
cored and roughly chopped

4 tbsp flour

1 tbsp vegetable oil

2 cloves garlic, crushed

2 onions, chopped

½ tsp dry mustard

2 tbsp chopped fresh parsley

2 tbsp Worcestershire sauce

1½ cups beef stock

2 tsp tomato paste

375g (13oz) prepared puff
pastry

2 tbsp milk

1 Place steak, kidneys and flour in a plastic food bag and shake to coat meat with flour. Shake off excess flour and set aside. Heat oil in a large skillet and cook meat over a high heat, stirring, until brown on all sides. Reduce heat to medium, add garlic and onions and cook for 3 minutes longer. Stir in mustard, parsley, Worcestershire sauce, stock and tomato paste, bring to simmering, cover and simmer, stirring occasionally, for 2½ hours or until meat is tender. Remove pan from heat and set aside to cool completely.

2 Place cooled filling in a 4-cup capacity pie dish. On a lightly floured surface, roll out pastry to 5cm (2in) larger than pie dish. Cut off a 1cm (⅓in) strip from pastry edge. Brush rim of dish with water and press pastry strip onto rim. Brush pastry strip with water. Lift pastry top over filling and press gently to seal edges. Trim and knock back edges to make a decorative edge. Brush with milk and bake for 30 minutes or until pastry is golden and crisp.

Serves 6

Breaded Lamb Chops with Parsnip Mash

Preparation 15 mins **Cooking** 20 mins **Calories** 804

2 tsp Dijon mustard
2 tsp clear honey
2 cloves garlic, crushed
1 tbsp chopped fresh rosemary, plus extra sprigs to garnish
3 tbsp olive oil or melted butter
salt and black pepper
8 lamb loin chops
100g (4oz) fine white fresh breadcrumbs

Parsnip Mash
500g (18oz) parsnips, cut into chunks
500g (18oz) floury potatoes, cut into chunks
2 cloves garlic
60g (2oz) butter
5 tbsp light cream
freshly grated nutmeg

Parsnip Mash

1 Cook the parsnips, potatoes and garlic in a saucepan of boiling salted water for 15–20 minutes, until tender. Drain well, then mash with the butter and cream until smooth. Season with salt, pepper and nutmeg.

Chops

1 Mix together the mustard, honey, garlic, rosemary and 2 tablespoons of the oil or butter. Season well with pepper. Thickly brush the mixture all over the chops, then coat with the breadcrumbs.

2 Meanwhile, preheat the broiler to medium-high. Place the chops on the broiler rack and drizzle with the remaining oil or butter. Broil for 7–8 minutes on each side, until tender (adjust the heat, if necessary, to ensure the breadcrumbs don't burn). Serve the chops with the mash and garnish with rosemary.

Serves 4

Note: The crunchy coating seals in the flavor of these rich lamb chops and goes beautifully with the sweet parsnip mash and a generous dollop of redcurrant preserve.

Beef in Beer

Preparation 15 mins **Cooking** 2½ hrs **Calories** 125

2 tbsp vegetable oil

750g (1¾lb) lean topside beef, cut into 25mm (1in) cubes

2 onions, chopped

2 carrots, cut into 1cm slices

2 tbsp flour

125ml (4fl oz) beer

500ml (1 pint) beef stock

2 cloves garlic, crushed

1 tbsp grated fresh ginger

2 tbsp honey

1 tbsp finely grated orange zest

freshly ground black pepper

1 Heat oil in a large nonstick skillet and cook beef over a high heat until browned on all sides. Transfer beef to a large ovenproof dish.

2 Reduce heat to medium and cook onions and carrots for 4–5 minutes or until onions start to soften. Stir in flour and cook for 1 minute, stirring continuously, then add beer and 125ml (4fl oz) stock and cook for 3–4 minutes, stirring to lift any sediment from base of pan. Stir in remaining stock, garlic, ginger, honey, orange zest and black pepper to taste.

3 Pour the remaining stock over meat, cover and cook for 1¾–2 hours or until meat is tender.

Serves 4

Thai Fried Noodles

Preparation 15 mins **Cooking** 15 mins **Calories** 157

vegetable oil for deep-frying
250g (9oz) rice vermicelli noodles
2 tsp sesame oil
2 onions, chopped
2 cloves garlic, crushed
200g (7oz) pork fillets, chopped
200g (7oz) boneless chicken breast fillets, chopped
1 tsp dried chili flakes
125g (4oz) bean sprouts
2 tbsp Thai fish sauce (nam pla)
1 tbsp lemon juice
2 tsp tamarind concentrate

1 Heat vegetable oil in a wok or large saucepan over a high heat until very hot. Deep-fry noodles, a few at a time, for 1–2 minutes or until lightly golden and puffed. Remove and set aside.

2 Heat sesame oil in a wok or skillet over a medium heat, add onions and garlic and stir-fry for 4 minutes or until soft and golden. Add pork, chicken and chili flakes and stir-fry for 4 minutes or until pork and chicken are brown and cooked.

3 Add bean sprouts, fish sauce, lemon juice, tamarind and noodles and stir-fry for 2 minutes or until heated through. Serve immediately.

Serves 4

Apricot and Citrus Glazed Chicken

Preparation 15 mins **Cooking** 45 mins **Calories** 427

4 chicken leg joints, about 250g (9oz) each

5 cups chicken stock

2 tbsp apricot preserve

30g (1oz) butter

finely grated zest of 1 orange and 1 lime or lemon

1–2 tsp light soy sauce

1 Place the chicken in a flameproof dish, cover with the stock or water and bring to the boil. Lower the heat, cover and simmer for 35 minutes or until the chicken is cooked through.

2 Warm the preserve in a saucepan for 1–2 minutes, then press through a sieve into a clean pan. Add the butter, orange and lime or lemon zest and heat for 1–2 minutes, until the butter has melted. Remove from the heat and stir in the soy sauce.

3 Preheat the broiler to high. Remove the chicken from the poaching liquid and pat dry with kitchen towels. Remove the gristle from the end of each drumstick. Place the chicken in the base of a broiler pan. Pour over the glaze and broil for 3–5 minutes, until golden brown and crisp.

Serves 4

Note: Citrus fruits and a glaze of apricot preserve give this gently poached chicken a sweet tangy flavor and a lovely crispy skin. Serve it with rice and shredded savoy cabbage.

Duck with Braised Turnips

Preparation 15 mins **Cooking** 50 mins **Calories** 450

4 duck leg joints
500g (18oz) white turnips, peeled and cut into 5cm (2in) chunks
salt and black pepper
½ cup chicken stock
1 tsp superfine sugar
1 tbsp fresh orange juice

1 Preheat the oven to 190°C (380°F). Heat a non-stick skillet, add the duck, skin-side down, then cook over a medium-high heat for 7–8 minutes, until browned. Pour off the fat that runs out and reserve it. Place the duck, skin-side up, on a baking sheet and cook for 30–40 minutes, until the skin is crisp and the meat cooked through.

2 Meanwhile, cook the turnips in boiling salted water for 5–6 minutes, until softened, then drain. Place 2 tablespoons of the reserved duck fat in a large skillet, add the turnips and fry for 5 minutes or until lightly browned. Add the stock and season.

3 Partly cover the pan and cook for 10 minutes or until the turnips are tender and almost all the liquid has evaporated. Uncover the pan, add the sugar and orange juice, then cook over a high heat for 3–4 minutes, stirring, until the turnips caramelize. Serve with the duck.

Serves 4

Chicken and Nectarine Salad

Preparation 10 mins **Cooking** none **Calories** 70

1 lettuce of your choice, leaves separated

1 bunch watercress, broken into sprigs

500g (18oz) cooked chicken, chopped

1 red capsicum, sliced

4 nectarines, sliced

2 stalks celery, sliced

Black Pepper Dressing

3 tsp crushed black peppercorns

1 tbsp olive oil

2 tbsp red wine vinegar

Chicken and Nectarine Salad

1 Arrange lettuce leaves, watercress, chicken, red capsicum, nectarines and celery in a salad bowl or on a large serving platter.

Black Pepper Dressing

1 Place black peppercorns, oil and vinegar in a screwtop jar and shake well to combine. Spoon dressing over salad and serve immediately.

Serves 4

Alternative: Use 400g (14oz) can apricots, drained or 10 fresh apricots, sliced, instead of the nectarine.

Skewered Chicken with Salsa

Preparation 25 mins + 15 mins standing **Cooking** 12 mins **Calories** 230

4 skinless boneless chicken breasts, cut into 25mm (1in) cubes
¼ tsp Tabasco
1 tbsp olive oil

Salsa

400g (14oz) can chopped tomatoes
2 cloves garlic, crushed
½ red onion or 1 small white onion, finely chopped
2 tsp mild chili powder
salt
large pinch of cayenne pepper
1 tbsp chopped fresh cilantro
1 tbsp olive oil
juice of ½ lemon

1 If using bamboo skewers, soak them in water for at least 10 minutes. Preheat the broiler to high. Thread the chicken evenly onto 4 skewers. Mix together the Tabasco and oil and brush over the chicken. Broil for 10–12 minutes, turning often, until the chicken is cooked through and tender. Serve with the salsa.

Salsa

1 Place the tomatoes, garlic, onion, chili powder, salt, cayenne pepper, cilantro and olive oil in a bowl and mix together well. Cover and leave to stand for 15 minutes for the flavors to develop, then add the lemon juice.

Serves 4

Note: You can make your own spicy Mexican salsa in minutes if you use canned tomatoes, and it really livens up these chicken kebabs. Serve them with tortilla french fries.

Parmesan Drumsticks

Preparation 10 mins **Cooking** 30 mins **Calories** 378

3 tbsp Dijon mustard
4 tbsp olive oil
4 scallions
30g (1oz) grated Parmesan cheese
freshly ground black pepper
8 chicken drumsticks
½ cup breadcrumbs, made from stale bread
3 tbsp melted butter

1 Place mustard, oil, scallions, Parmesan cheese and black pepper (to taste), in a bowl and mix to combine.

2 Brush each drumstick with mustard mixture, then roll in the breadcrumbs and place in a lightly greased baking dish. Pour butter over drumsticks and bake at 180°C (350°F) for 30 minutes or until drumsticks are cooked.

Note: Crispy on the outside and moist on the inside, these drumsticks are a popular family meal. Serve with mashed potatoes and a green salad for one of the easiest meals you will ever make.

Roast Chicken with Corn and Ham Fritters

Preparation 15 mins + 15 mins standing **Cooking** 1 hr 25 mins **Calories** 607

small whole chicken, about
1 kg (2¼ lb)

juice of ½ lemon

2 large cloves garlic, halved

1 small onion, quartered

salt and black pepper

1 tsp paprika

2 tbsp olive oil

Fritters

2 medium eggs

4 tbsp whole milk

100g (4oz) flour

¼ tsp baking soda

salt

200g (7oz) can corn, drained

95g (3oz) ham, finely chopped

vegetable oil for frying

Chicken

1 Preheat the oven to 200°C (400°F). Rinse the chicken inside and out, then pat dry with kitchen towels. Sprinkle the inside of the chicken with lemon juice, then place the garlic, onion and seasoning in the cavity. Place in a roasting tin, sprinkle with paprika, then drizzle over the oil. Roast for 1–1¼ hours, basting 2–3 times during cooking. Check that it is cooked by inserting a skewer into the thigh; the juices should run clear. Rest, covered in aluminum foil, for 15 minutes before carving.

Fritters

2 Meanwhile, make the fritters. Beat together the eggs, milk, flour and baking soda with a little salt until smooth. Stir in the corn and ham. Heat 5mm (¼ in) of oil in a deep heavy-based skillet and drop in large spoonfuls of the mixture to make fritters. Cook the fritters for 1–2 minutes on each side, until crisp and golden (you may have to do this in batches) and serve with the chicken.

Serves 4

Note: Succulent roast chicken is always a winner. But if you want to do something a bit different, serve it with these crunchy fritters and some green beans.

Chicken Stroganoff

Preparation 8 mins **Cooking** 18 mins **Calories** 335

2 tbsp olive oil
1 onion, sliced
1 clove garlic, crushed
8 chicken thigh fillets or
4 boneless chicken breast
fillets, sliced
125g (4oz) white mushrooms,
sliced
1¼ cups sour cream
¼ cup tomato purée
½ tsp paprika
freshly ground black pepper
2 scallions, chopped or
chopped fresh parsley

1 Heat oil in a skillet over a medium heat, add onion and garlic and cook, stirring, for 4–5 minutes or until onion is tender. Add chicken and cook, stirring, for 3–4 minutes or until chicken is just cooked. Add mushrooms and cook, stirring, for 2 minutes longer.

2 Stir sour cream, tomato purée, paprika and black pepper to taste into the pan, bring to simmering and simmer for 5 minutes or until sauce thickens. Sprinkle with scallions or parsley and serve immediately.

Serves 6

Note: Chicken is a cheaper choice for protein and works just as well as red meat in classic dishes such as this. Serve with rice or pasta and a green salad.

Variation: Add 400g (14oz) canned undrained, mashed tomatoes with the mushrooms.

Moules Marinières

Preparation 20 mins **Cooking** 20 mins **Calories** 218

2kg (4½lb) fresh mussels
2 onions, chopped
3 shallots, chopped
2 tbsp chopped fresh parsley, plus extra to garnish
⅗ cup white wine or fish stock
4 tbsp heavy cream
salt and black pepper

Variation: To vary this dish, use 60g (2oz) butter, 200g (7oz) sliced mushrooms, 100g (4oz) diced bacon and 2 stalks celery sliced instead of parsley and shallots. These ingredients should be added with the onions, water, wine or stock.

1 Scrub the mussels under cold running water, then pull away any beards and discard any mussels that are open or damaged.

2 Put the onions, shallots, parsley, ⅗ cup of water, and the wine or stock in a large heavy-based saucepan. Cook gently for 10 minutes or until the onions and shallots have softened. Add the mussels, then cover and cook for 5 minutes or until the shells have opened, shaking the pan from time to time. Place a colander over a bowl and strain the mussels. Reserve the cooking liquid and discard any mussels that remain closed.

3 Pour the reserved liquid into the pan and boil for 5 minutes or until reduced by half. Remove from the heat and stir in the cream. Season if necessary. Return to the heat and warm through, but do not boil. Divide the mussels between 4 large bowls, pour over the sauce and sprinkle with parsley.

Serves 4

Note: Fresh mussels with a cream and white wine sauce make a really impressive dish. Serve them with warm crusty bread to soak up the delicious juices.

Blackened Red Snapper with Crème Fraîche

Preparation 15 mins **Cooking** 10 mins **Calories** 185

125g (4oz) unsalted butter

125ml (4fl oz) freshly squeezed lemon juice

¼ tsp each salt, ground cayenne pepper, garlic powder, and onion powder

½ tsp dried thyme leaves

1kg (2¼lb) red snapper fillets

125g (4oz) crème fraîche

1 Melt butter in a small saucepan over low heat. Stir in lemon juice, salt, cayenne pepper, garlic powder, onion powder and thyme. Pour the seasoned butter into a shallow dish.

2 Heat a large, heavy skillet over high heat. Roll the red snapper in the seasoned butter, and fry it quickly, turning it once (for about 2 minutes on each side). The red snapper will char on the outside and be tender on the inside. With a spatula, transfer the fish to a heated platter.

3 Place the fish on individual plates and serve it hot with a spoonful of crème fraîche.

Serves 6

Variation: This dish may also be prepared using prepared blackening spices in place of the above seasonings.

Tandoori Cod with Cucumber and Carrot Raita

Preparation 20 mins + 4 hrs marinating **Cooking** 8 mins **Calories** 209

145g (5oz) plain yogurt
1 tsp mild chili powder
1 tsp paprika
1 tsp ground cumin
½ tsp ground cilantro
½ tsp turmeric
1 tsp garam masala
1 large clove garlic, crushed
1 tsp tomato paste
juice of ½ lime
680g (1½ lb)skinless cod fillet, cut into 4 pieces

Raita

¼ cucumber, grated
1 carrot, grated
145g (5oz) carton plain yogurt
2 tbsp chopped fresh mint or cilantro

Raita

1 Pat dry the cucumber, using absorbent paper, and mix together with the carrot, yogurt and mint or cilantro. Cover and refrigerate until needed. Preheat the broiler to high. Place the marinated cod in a roasting tin or shallow flameproof dish. Place under the broiler and cook for 8 minutes or until the flesh is firm and cooked through, turning once. Serve the cod with the raita.

Cod

1 Mix together the yogurt, chili powder, paprika, cumin, cilantro, turmeric, garam masala, garlic, tomato paste and lime juice. Place the cod in a large, shallow, non-metallic dish. Pour over the marinade and turn to cover all of the fish. Cover and refrigerate for 4 hours or overnight, turning occasionally.

Serves 4

Salmon Koulibiac

Preparation 25 mins + hr 15 mins cooling **Cooking** 1 hr **Calories** 639

90g (3oz) long-grain rice
2 medium eggs
1 tbsp oil
1 onion, finely chopped
1 tbsp chopped fresh parsley
50g (2oz) mushrooms, finely chopped
juice of ½ lemon
salt and black pepper
370g (13oz) pack ready-rolled puff pastry
400g (14oz) can salmon, drained and flaked
milk for brushing

Variation: You can use 400g (14oz) canned tuna instead of the salmon to vary this dish.

1 Preheat the oven to 200°C (400°). Cook the rice according to the instructions on the packet, then drain. Set aside for 1 hour or until completely cooled. Meanwhile, boil the eggs for 10 minutes, then peel under cold running water and chop. Heat the oil in a skillet, add the onion and cook for 5 minutes or until softened. Add the parsley and mushrooms and cook for 3–4 minutes. Stir in the lemon juice and season.

2 Roll out the pastry to extend the shorter side to 30cm (12in). Cut to make 2 rectangles, one 12 x 30cm (5in x12in), the other 24 x 30cm (9¼in x 12in). Place the smaller piece on a baking tray, prick with a fork and cook for 10 minutes or until lightly golden. Leave to cool for 15 minutes.

3 Combine the onion mixture, rice, eggs and salmon, then place down the center of the baked pastry. Trim the corners from the unbaked pastry and lay it over the top. Dampen the edges, tuck under the pastry base and press to seal. Score the top, brush with milk and cook for 25–30 min (9 ¼in) utes, until golden.

Serves 4

Note: This variation on a Russian Pie uses canned salmon, but you could use lightly poached tail end fillets instead.

Fish Cakes with Tartar Sauce

Preparation 35 mins + 1 hr chiling **Cooking** 50 mins **Calories** 726

500g (18oz) potatoes, cut into chunks
salt and black pepper
500g (18oz) cod fillets
⅘ cup whole milk
2 tbsp chopped fresh parsley
4 scallions, finely sliced
4 tbsp flour
2 medium eggs, beaten
90g (3oz) dried breadcrumbs
oil for shallow frying

Tartar Sauce
6 tbsp mayonnaise
2 tbsp crème fraîche
1 tbsp capers, rinsed, dried and chopped
2 tbsp finely chopped gherkins
1 tbsp chopped fresh parsley
1 tbsp chopped fresh tarragon
½ tsp finely grated lemon zest

Fish Cakes

1 Cook the potatoes in boiling salted water for 15 minutes or until tender. Drain, then mash and leave to cool. Meanwhile, place the fish in a skillet and pour over the milk. Cook over a low heat, partly covered, for 10 minutes or until just cooked. Remove from the milk and flake, discarding any skin or bones.

2 Mix together the fish, mashed potatoes, parsley and scallions and season well. Shape into 8 cakes, 2cm (1in) thick. Season the flour with salt and pepper. Dip the fish cakes into the seasoned flour, then the beaten egg, and finally the breadcrumbs, coating well. Refrigerate for 1 hour.

3 Heat 5mm (1¼in) oil in a skillet and fry half the fish cakes for 5–6 minutes on each side, until golden. Drain on absorbent paper, then keep warm while you cook the rest. Serve with the tartar sauce.

Tartar Sauce

1 Mix the mayonnaise with the crème fraîche, capers, gherkins, herbs, lemon zest and pepper.

Serves 4

Sole with Creamed Cucumber Sauce

Preparation 15 mins + 1 hr standing **Cooking** 50 mins **Calories** 615

125g (4oz) unsalted butter
5 tbsp flour
salt and black pepper
8 sole fillets
lemon slices to serve

Cucumber Sauce

1 cucumber, peeled, halved lengthways, deseeded and sliced
1 tsp salt
30g (1oz) butter
2 shallots, finely chopped
4 tbsp white wine vinegar
4 tbsp dry white wine
4 tbsp heavy cream
2 tsp chopped fresh tarragon

Sole

1 Place the cucumber in a colander and sprinkle with salt, tossing to mix. Leave to stand for 1 hour, then rinse and dry. Melt the unsalted butter in a saucepan over a low heat and bubble for 3–4 minutes without browning. Line a sieve with damp muslin, place over a bowl and carefully pour in the butter, discarding the milky deposit left in the pan. Leave the strained liquid (clarified butter) to cool.

2 Season the flour with salt and pepper, then coat the fish in the mixture. Heat the clarified butter in a skillet, then fry half the fish for 3–5 minutes on each side, until golden. Drain on absorbent paper, then keep warm while you cook the remaining fish. Serve with the cucumber sauce and lemon slices.

Cucumber Sauce

1 Heat the butter in a saucepan, add the shallots and cook for 5 minutes to soften. Add the cucumber and fry for 10 minutes, stirring occasionally. Stir in the vinegar and wine, and cook briskly for 5–8 minutes, until only 1–2 tablespoons of liquid remain in the pan. Add the cream and tarragon and heat for 1–2 minutes. Season.

Serves 4

Stir-Fried Shrimp Salad

Preparation 25 mins **Cooking** 5 mins **Calories** 82

16 uncooked shrimp, shelled and de-veined, tails left intact

1 fresh green chili, seeded and shredded

3 tbsp soy sauce

1 tbsp honey

1 endive, leaves separated

1 radicchio, leaves separated

2 green (unripe) mangoes, thinly sliced

4 tbsp fresh mint leaves

3 tbsp fresh cilantro leaves

1 tbsp brown sugar

2 tbsp lime juice

1 Place shrimp, chili, soy sauce and honey in a bowl, toss to combine and marinate for 5 minutes.

2 Arrange the endive, radicchio, mangoes, mint and cilantro on serving plates. Combine sugar and lime juice and drizzle over salad.

3 Heat a nonstick skillet over a high heat, add the shrimps and stir-fry for 2 minutes or until cooked. Place the shrimp on top of salad, spoon over pan juices and serve immediately.

Serves 4

Mixed Vegetable Cheese Bake

Preparation 30 mins **Cooking** 1 hr 20 mins **Calories** 477

1 large butternut squash, peeled, deseeded and cut into chunks

salt and black pepper

3 tbsp olive oil

1 large cauliflower, cut into florets

340g (12oz) mushrooms, sliced

2 tbsp fresh white breadcrumbs

2 tbsp freshly shredded Parmesan cheese

Sauce

30g (1oz) butter, plus extra for greasing

30g (1oz) flour

pinch of cayenne pepper

1⅓ cups whole milk

1 tsp English mustard

100g Cheddar cheese, shredded

1 Preheat the oven to 200°C (400°). Put the squash into an ovenproof dish, season, then drizzle over ½ the oil. Roast for 25 minutes, stirring once, until squash is tender. Meanwhile, cook the cauliflower in boiling salted water for 5 minutes or until just tender. Drain, reserving 200ml (7fl oz) of the cooking water, then refresh in cold water and set aside. Fry the mushrooms in the remaining oil for 4–5 minutes.

2 Reduce the oven temperature. Add the cauliflower to the squash, then divide between 4 individual ovenproof dishes. Scatter over the mushrooms and pour over the sauce. Mix the breadcrumbs and Parmesan cheese together, then sprinkle over each dish. Bake for 30–35 minutes.

Sauce

1 Melt the butter in a saucepan and stir in the flour and cayenne pepper. Cook for 2 minutes, then gradually stir in the reserved cooking liquid. Cook for 2–3 minutes, until thick, then gradually stir in the milk. Simmer, stirring, for 10 minutes. Remove from the heat, then stir in the mustard and the cheese, until melted. Season to taste.

Serves 4

Corn and Mushroom Roulade

Preparation 30 mins + 10 mins cooling **Cooking** 45 mins **Calories** 364

75g (2½oz) butter, plus extra for greasing

125g (4oz) mushrooms, chopped

75g (2½oz) flour

⅗ cup vegetable stock

125g (4oz) canned or frozen corn, drained or defrosted

170ml (6fl oz) milk

4 medium eggs, separated

Pepper Sauce

1 red capsicum, deseeded and halved

2 tomatoes

145ml (5fl oz) strained plain yogurt

salt and black pepper

Capiscum Sauce

1 Roast the capsicum for 20 minutes. Cool for 10 minutes, then skin and chop. Cover the tomatoes with boiling water and leave for 30 seconds. Peel, deseed and chop, then combine with the yogurt and seasoning.

Roulade

1 Preheat oven to 200°C (400°F). Melt ¼ of the butter in a saucepan, then fry the mushrooms for 3–4 minutes. Add ¼ of the flour, stir for 1 minute, then remove from the heat and gradually stir in the stock. Return to the heat and simmer, stirring, for 1–2 minutes, until thickened. Add the corn and keep warm. Grease a 25 x 30cm (10x12in) swiss roll tin and line with baking paper.

2 Melt the remaining butter in a pan and stir in the rest of the flour. Cook for 1 minute, then remove from the heat and slowly stir in the milk. Bring to the boil, stirring. Cool slightly, then beat in the egg yolks. Beat the whites until stiff, then fold into the yolk mixture. Pour into the tin, then cook for 15 minutes or until golden. Turn out and peel off the lining. Spread over the filling, then roll up and serve with the sauce.

Serves 4

Note: Serve this light roulade and pepper sauce with a mixed salad, or on its own as an impressive starter.

Baby Eggplant with Ginger and Sweet Soy

Preparation 15 mins **Cooking** 15 mins **Calories** 39

8 baby eggplants
vegetable oil
3 cloves garlic, crushed
1 tbsp grated fresh ginger
1 tsp cumin seeds
pinch chili powder
1 tbsp sweet soy sauce
2 tbsp lemon juice
¼ cup basil leaves

1 Cut the eggplants in half, leaving the stems attached. Brush the cut sides lightly with the oil.

2 Heat a large non-stick skillet over a medium heat and add the eggplants, cut side down, and cook until they start to soften and turn golden. Remove.

3 Add the garlic, ginger, cumin, chili powder and 1 tablespoon water to the pan and cook until the garlic is soft.

4 Stir in the soy sauce, lemon juice and ½ cup water and bring to a low simmer. Return the eggplants to the pan and cook for 10 minutes, or until soft and most of the liquid has been absorbed. Transfer to serving plates and top with basil leaves.

Serves 4–6

Asian Greens with Sweet Soy and Sesame Dressing

Preparation 5 mins **Cooking** 5 mins **Calories** 113

500g (18oz) baby bok choi
500g (18oz) Chinese broccoli
285g (10oz) water spinach
½ tsp sesame oil
1 tbsp oyster sauce
1 tbsp sweet soy sauce
1 tbsp rice vinegar
1 tbsp sesame seeds, toasted

1 Cut the bok choi, Chinese broccoli and spinach into 20cm (8in) lengths. Wash, drain and put in a large bamboo steamer lined with baking paper. Cook over a wok of simmering water, making sure the base of the steamer does not come in contact with the water, for 5 minutes or until vegetables are bright green and tender.

2 Beat together the sesame oil, oyster sauce, say sauce and rice vinegar in a jug.

3 Neatly pile the vegetables onto a serving plate and drizzle with the sauce. Sprinkle with sesame seeds and serve.

Serves 4

Creamy Potato Gratin

Preparation 15 mins **Cooking** 45 mins **Calories** 243

680g (1½lb) waxy potatoes
1 onion, thinly sliced
1½ cups evaporated milk
½ cup chicken stock
½ cup shredded Cheddar cheese

1 Preheat the oven to 180°C (350°). Peel the potatoes and cut into thin slices. Layer the potato and onion in a 6-cup capacity ovenproof dish.

2 Beat together the evaporated milk, chicken stock and ½ the cheese. Pour over the layered potatoes.

3 Sprinkle with the cheese and bake, covered, for 30 minutes then uncovered for 15 minutes or until the potato is tender and the cheese is golden.

Serves 4–6

Mixed Beans with Pine Nuts and Parmesan

Preparation 10 mins **Cooking** 10 mins **Calories** 146

250g (9oz) yellow beans, trimmed

200g (7oz) green beans, trimmed

2 tbsp red wine vinegar

1 tsp honey

1 clove garlic, crushed

2 tbsp fresh mint, finely sliced

1 tbsp mustard seed oil

2 tbsp pine nuts, toasted

2 tbsp shaved Parmesan cheese

cracked black pepper to taste

1   Steam or microwave the beans until tender. Do not overcook or they will lose their color. Drain well.

2   Beat together the red wine vinegar, honey, garlic, mint and mustard seed oil in a small jug.

3   Pour the dressing over the beans and top with the toasted pine nuts, Parmesan cheese and cracked black pepper.

Serves 4

Individual Macaroni, Broccolini and Cauliflower Cheese

Preparation 20 mins **Cooking** 30 mins **Calories** 182

55g (2oz) macaroni
250g (9oz) cauliflower, cut into florets
250g (9oz) broccolini or broccoli, cut into florets
1 tbsp butter
1 tbsp flour
pinch saffron
pinch nutmeg
1 cup evaporated milk
⅓ cup shredded Cheddar cheese

1 Preheat oven to 200°C (400°F). Lightly grease four 1-cup ramekins.

2 Cook the macaroni in a large pot of rapidly boiling water until al dente (cooked, but still firm to the bite). Drain well and set aside.

3 Steam or microwave the cauliflower and broccolini or broccoli separately until tender. Rinse under cold water and drain well.

4 Heat the butter in a small pan, add the flour, saffron and nutmeg and cook, stirring constantly, until bubbling. Remove from the heat and gradually stir in the milk.

5 Return the pan to the heat and bring to the boil, stirring constantly until the sauce boils and thickens. Reduce the heat and simmer for 5 minutes.

6 Put the macaroni in the base of the ramekins, top with the combined cauliflower and broccolini and pour over the sauce. Sprinkle with cheese. Bake for 15 minutes or until the sauce is golden and bubbling.

Serves 4

Bakewell Tart with Plums

Preparation 20 mins + 30 mins chiling **Cooking** 1 hr 15 mins **Calories** 751

170g (6oz) flour
45g (1½oz) superfine sugar
85g (3oz) butter, diced
1 medium egg yolk
juice of ½ lemon

Filling

500g (18oz) plums, halved, stoned and chopped
170g (6oz) superfine sugar
125g (4oz) sweetened butter, softened
2 medium eggs, beaten
145g (5oz) ground almonds
few drops almond extract (optional)
1 tbsp flaked almonds

Pastry Case

1   Sift the flour and sugar into a bowl, add the butter and rub in using your fingertips until the mixture resembles fine breadcrumbs. Add the egg yolk and lemon juice and mix to a dough. Cover and refrigerate for 30 minutes.

2   Preheat the oven to 190°C (380°F). Use the pastry to line a deep 20cm metal flan tin. Line with baking paper and baking beans, then bake blind for 10–12 minutes, until the pastry is golden. Discard baking beans, set aside, then reduce the oven temperature to 180°C (350°F).

Filling

1   Cook the plums with 55g (2oz) of sugar in a saucepan for 10 minutes or until soft. Cool, drain, discarding the syrup, then spread plums over the pastry case. Beat the butter and remaining sugar together until light and fluffy. Beat in the eggs a little at a time, then beat in the ground almonds and extract if using. Smooth the filling over the plums, sprinkle with the flaked almonds, then bake for 50 minutes or until the filling is set.

Serves 6

Note: This tart was originally known as Bakewell pudding and it proves that old-fashioned things are sometimes the best.

Treacle Tart

Preparation 15 mins **Cooking** 40 mins **Calories** 487

500g (18oz) short pastry,
defrosted if frozen

Filling

500g (18oz) can corn syrup

100g (4oz) fresh white
breadcrumbs

1 tsp ground ginger

finely grated rind of
1 lemon and juice of ½ lemon

2 eating apples, peeled, cored
and coarsely grated

*Alternative: In order to
change this recipe you could
replace the ingredients with
1 egg, ½ cup maple syrup,
zest of ½ orange, 60g (2oz)
caster sugar, 60g (60oz)
butter and 125g (4oz)
butter. Whisk the egg witth
the maple syrup, orange
zest, sugar and butter until
blended. Pour into pastry case
and arrange pecans on top.
Bake for 30 minutes.
Allow to cool*

Filling

1   Open the can of syrup and place the full can
in a saucepan. Pour in boiling water to reach
halfway up the side of the can. Warm over a
low heat for 5 minutes or until the syrup is very
runny. Place the breadcrumbs, ginger, lemon
rind and juice and apples in a bowl. Pour over
the syrup and mix.

Pastry Case

1   Preheat the oven to 190°C (380°F). Roll out
the pastry on a lightly floured surface and use
to line a 20cm (8in) flan tin at least 2½cm (1in)
deep. Trim off the excess pastry and reserve for
decoration. Line with baking paper and baking
beans, then bake blind for 10–12 minutes, until
the pastry is lightly golden. Remove the paper
and beans.

2   Pour the filling into the pastry case. Roll out the
reserved pastry and cut into strips, then twist gently.
Lay the strips in a criss-cross pattern on top of the
tart. Bake for 25–30 minutes, until bubbling.

Serves 6

*Note: Corn syrup is used rather than molasses,
or treacle these days, but the pudding has kept
its name. Serve with vanilla ice cream.*

Fragrant Baked Pears

Preparation 25 mins **Cooking** 30 mins **Calories** 169

3 firm ripe pears, peeled
4 cinnamon sticks
2 whole cloves
1½ tsp ground cinnamon
½ tsp ground nutmeg
2 tbsp sweetened butter, cut into cubes
¾ cup dark rum or orange juice
4 tbsp brown sugar
cream, to serve

1 Halve the pears lengthways and remove the cores. Place them cut side down on a board and cut each half crosswise into 5 or 6 even slices, being careful to retain the shape of the pear.

2 Place the pears into a buttered baking dish and fan the slices out a little.

3 Put the cinnamon sticks and cloves into the dish and sprinkle each pear with the sugar, cinnamon and nutmeg.

4 Dot the pears with the butter and bake for 20–25 minutes at 175°C (340°F).

5 Remove the pears from the oven and pour over the rum or orange juice and return to the oven for 5 minutes.

6 Serve warm, with cream.

Serves 6

Key Lime Pie

Preparation 30 mins **Cooking** 50 mins + chiling time **Calories** 452

Syrup

1 cup water
½ cup sugar
2 tbsp grated lime zest

Crumb Crust

2 cups plain sweet biscuit crumbs
200g (7oz) butter, melted
2 tsp grated lime zest

Filling

1 envelope unflavored gelatin
⅓ cup fresh lime juice
½ cup superfine sugar
2 eggs, separated
1 cup cream
1 tsp vanilla essence

Syrup

1 Combine the water and sugar in a small saucepan and heat to a simmer. Stir in the lime zest and simmer for 30 minutes.

Crumb Crust

1 Combine all ingredients in a bowl, mix well and press over base of 24cm (9in) greased spring form tin. Bake at 180°C (350°F) for 8 minutes.

Filling

1 Heat ⅓ cup of the reserved lime syrup in a small saucepan. Remove from heat and sprinkle gelatin over the syrup and let soften for 1 minute.

2 Stir in the lime juice, ¼ cup of sugar and the 2 egg yolks. Stir over low heat until mixture is thick and frothy, about 5 minutes. Set aside to cool.

3 Beat egg whites and 2 tablespoons of sugar until stiff. In another bowl beat the cream, vanilla and remaining 2 tablespoons of sugar until thick.

4 Fold the cream into the egg whites, drizzling the reserved lime mixture at the same time. When the mixture is smooth spoon into the prepared crust. Chill until firm, 2–3 hours.

Serves 8

Apple Fritters

Preparation 15 mins **Cooking** 10 mins **Calories** 300

4 desert apples, peeled, cored and sliced into 5mm (½in) rings

2 eggs

1 tbsp sugar

3 tbsp flour

pinch salt

vegetable oil for deep frying

superfine sugar

1 Mix together the eggs, sugar, flour and salt.

2 Heat enough oil to come up 1½cm (¾in) in the skillet.

3 Dip the apple pieces into batter and fry them in the hot oil.

4 Drain the pieces on absorbent paper and then serve them sprinkled with superfine sugar.

Serves 4

Apple Crumble

Preparation 15 mins **Cooking** 1 hr **Calories** 229

5 Desert apples, peeled, cored and thinly sliced

2 tbsp fresh lemon juice

1 cup flour

1 cup sugar

1½ tsp cinnamon

125g (4oz) butter, cold, cut into pieces

cream, ice cream or custard, to serve

1 Place a layer of apples into a 20cm (8in) cake pan or baking dish and sprinkle with some of the lemon juice. Repeat the layers until all the apples are in the pan.

2 Process the flour, sugar and cinnamon in a blender and combine. Add the butter, using repeated pulses until the mixture resembles coarse breadcrumbs.

3 Sprinkle the crumb mixture over the apples.

4 Bake for 1 hour at 175°C (340°F). Serve warm with cream, ice cream or custard.

Serves 6

Fruity Fresh Plum Toasties

Preparation 10 mins **Cooking** 5 mins **Calories** 211

4 thick slices fruit bread,
brioche, cinnamon bread or
chollah

1–2 tbsp plum preserve

¼ tsp ground cinnamon

30g (1oz) superfine sugar

8–12 ripe red plums, halved
and stoned

*Variation: Use 250g (9oz)
strawberries and 2 tbsps of
strawberry preserve instead of
the plums and plum preserve.*

1 Preheat the broiler to high. Toast the bread slices
very lightly on both sides. Spread one side of
the toast with the preserve, then place the slices
in a single layer in a flameproof dish, preserve-
side up.

2 Mix together the cinnamon and sugar. Arrange
the plums on top of the toast and sprinkle with
the cinnamon sugar. Place under the broiler and
cook for 2–3 minutes, until the sugar begins
to melt and the plums are warmed through.
Leave to cool slightly before serving.

Serves 4

*Note: This is a great way of using up some
leftover fruit bread. Serve with a spoonful of
strained plain yogurt or crème fraîche, to serve.*

Dates Stuffed with Almonds

Preparation 15 mins **Cooking** 15 mins **Calories** 24

25 large dates, slit lengthways
on one side, stones removed

25 blanched almonds

200g (7oz) sugar

1 Toast the almonds by spreading them on a
baking sheet and placing them in a pre-heated
150°C (300°F) oven for about 15 minutes or
until a pale golden color. Then remove from
oven and allow to cool.

2 Place an almond into the slit in each date and
place the fruits on a wire rack placed on an
oven tray lined with baking paper.

3 Put the sugar in a small saucepan and place
over a medium heat and allow the sugar to
cook to a light amber color.

4 Immediately dribble a teaspoonful of the hot
caramel over each date to cover the almond.

5 Allow to cool and if not using immediately, store
in a tightly sealed container.

*Note: These tasty dates make a delightful and
different confectionery to serve with after-dinner
coffee.*

Index